The Ultimate Guide To Castlevania

By BlackNES Guy

STOP!!   BEFORE GOING ANY FURTHER...

...

Think you know everything about Super Mario Bros?

Download our FREE *Ultimate Guide to Super Mario Bros.* A look inside the pipes... At the History, Super Cheats, and Secret Levels
Of one of the most iconic video games in history.

Go here to get a FREE digital copy
http://bit.ly/supermarioguide

A Letter from BlackNES Guy

First I want to thank you for purchasing my book. Whether this is your first purchase or another one to add to your collection, I appreciate your choice. Let me introduce myself, I am the one and only BlackNES Guy, I am your average lover of video games, especially the retro games that I grew up with as a kid. When I play those games now, I think back to a simpler time when it was just me and my brother playing Super Mario World for the first time, or trying to figure out how to conquer The Legend of Zelda (without the help of the internet)! Playing those games now allows me to go back in time so to speak and relive some of those precious memories. Now being older and starting a family, I want to give my daughter the same type of experience, that is why I have created these books. They are for her as much as they are for you and me. They are designed to be a nostalgic collectable for the hardcore gamer or a simple 'old school' strategy guide to help you conquer that one game that has been eluding you all these years. Whatever your reason for buying theses books it is my goal that they help and serve you on your quest in whichever game it might be.

I have put together some additional bonuses for you inside this book. One is I invite you to join my **Facebook group**. Here we can connect and talk about retro games to our hearts content. I also love hearing any feedback you have on how to make the books even better or what guide you would like to see next! I have also included a **FREE digital download** of one of my books as a thank you for purchasing this one. You can get that by following the instructions on the next few pages. Lastly I want to tell you about my **Player 2 Press Start** team. The Player 2 Press Start team is my advance reading team. They get advance copies of my books before they are released to the public. They help make sure the book is in tip top shape by providing any additional thoughts or improvements before it goes live to the world. The most important part of being a Player 2, is when the book comes out, they leave a review on the Amazon page. Reviews are the lifeblood of my books, they let others know what you think of them. So its their job to leave reviews as soon as possible so others know how great the books are. If you want to join this team there is a link at the end of the book for you to sign up.

This is my way of giving back and adding some value to the gaming community. Video games have always been such an important part of my life and most likely yours too so I hope you enjoy my books and share them with all your gaming friends as well.

I would love to connect with you on social media as well, that info will be below :)

Thank you so much for choosing to invest your time in them.

Much love and Game On!

BlackNES Guy

Follow me on:
Twitter @blacknesguy
Facebook @ www.facebook.com/theBlackNESguy

For more great books check out my author page

www.theblacknesguy.com

More books by BlackNES Guy:

The Ultimate Guide to the NES Classic
The Ultimate Guide to Super Mario Bros
The Ultimate Guide to Super Mario Run
The Ultimate Guide to The Legend Of Zelda
The Ultimate Guide to The Legend Of Zelda 2
The Ultimate Guide To Castlevania
The Diary of Super Mario Bros Series

INTRODUCTION

To make the most of any game, you should know what moves you can do and what items and objects can help you on your quest!

CONTROLS & MOVES

B Button (leftmost action button): Jump. If you jump in the air without moving left or right, you won't be able to control your mid-air movement. Start your movement before jumping if you wish to jump in a certain direction.

A Button (rightmost action button): Attack in the direction you're facing

Up + A Button: Throwable weapon attack

Down: Duck. You can duck and attack at the same time. You can also jump and attack at the same time.

Moving on Stairs: To move onto and off of stairs, hold up at the bottom of the stairs, and down at the top of the stairs.

THE WEAPONS

Weapon: This is the item that is in the Weapon Indicator window right under the Time Remaining indicator. There are many weapons listed below. You can use this weapon as many times as you have Hearts, which are collected by destroying Creatures and Candlesticks.

All throwable weapons do damage as soon as they're thrown. That means that even as they're traveling through the air, they will destroy fireballs (and move through them) until they hit a Creature.

Magic Whip: This is the weapon that you start with. You can use it an unlimited number of times. You can also upgrade this weapon. Each time you pick up a **Morning Star**, you'll upgrade it to the next level. The original Magic Whip that you start with is the weakest whip. The first time you pick up the Morning Star, you'll upgrade the attack power of your Whip. While you have the Morning Star and pick up another one, you'll upgrade the length of your Whip.

	Damage	*Length*
MAGIC WHIP	+	+
MORNING STAR	++	+
MORNING STAR +	++	++

Fire Bomb: Throw a bomb and a fire will ignite wherever it lands. The splash will damage any enemies that come into contact with it. This is an excellent weapon to use against Bosses because they'll freeze in place and continue to be damaged by the fire. *Note: many players think that this bomb resembles a glass of Holy Water!*

Axe: Throw an Axe and it'll fly forwards in an arc. It's useful for attacking Creatures that might be above you. Slow but powerful.

Dagger: Throw a Dagger and it'll shoot forwards in a straight line. It'll damage any Creatures that it hits.

Watch: Use the Watch and time will pause: most Creatures will be frozen momentarily. Useful for quick enemies that are hard to hit. It'll cost 5 Hearts each time you use it.

Boomerang: Throw the Boomerang and it'll fly forwards in a straight line across to the edge of the screen before returning in the opposite direction. If you're in the flight path, it'll stop where you are, but you won't get any Hearts back. The major advantage of the Boomerang is that it'll pass through both fireballs and Creatures, and it'll do damage to Creatures on both ways.

THE ITEMS

Items are things you can pick up in the environment that'll help you in your quest to destroy the Count. Most of them drop from whatever you destroy, like enemies or parts of the level. Picking them up immediately activates it.

Hearts: These pickups are the number of times you can use your Weapon. Little Hearts give you 1 heart, and Big Hearts give you 5.

Invisibility Potion: This gold jug will make you invincible for a few seconds.

Morning Star: As described above in the Weapons section, this upgrades your Magic Whip.

Cross: This protective amulet destroys all the enemies on the screen in a flash.

Money Bag: This bag of money gives you more points depending on the color. Red gives you 100, Blue gives 400, and White gives 700. There are many Secret Tips throughout the game where you'll be given a chance to get a free Money Bag.

Double Shot and **Triple Shot**: This glowing stone tablet allows you to throw weapons two or three times in a row. You can also find these when you hit or destroy objects with your weapon 10 times in a row without missing. If you miss your shot and don't hit anything, you'll have to start counting from 0.

Pork Chop: This delicious piece of meat is usually hidden in walls and platforms. Pick it up and eat it to restore some of your health.

WALKTHROUGH

There are a total of 18 stages, and some stages will have separate rooms that you'll transition into through a staircase or door.

Stage 1

You start the adventure right outside the gates of the castle. You'll automatically enter and you take control in the courtyard.

The castle doors are to the right. Use your Magic Whip to destroy the 5 flaming fountains on the way to the door. You'll obtain two Morning Stars, which fully upgrades your whip.

You'll see the castle doors. Enter, if you dare!

Secret Tip

For an extra 1000 points, jump across the doorway instead of walking into it. A
Money Bag will come out of the ground to the left of the doorway where you just

came from! Remember to jump across the doorway on the way back to get it. Then continue by walking right, in through the door.

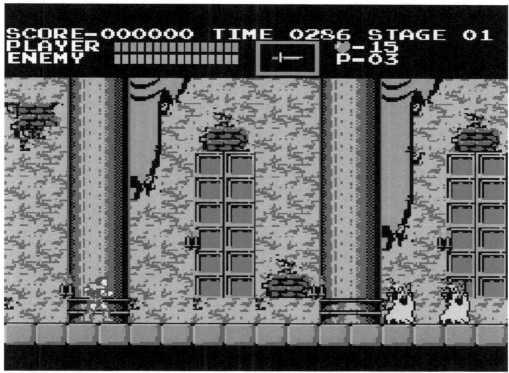

Once inside the castle, make your way to the right. Make sure to destroy all the Candlesticks to pick up the goodies.

Soon, you'll encounter your first set of stairs with a Black Leopard lying in wait. It'll pounce once you get close, so be careful—it'll land on the ground and run in your direction. Once you're safe, take this time to get familiar with how to move onto and off of the stairs.

You'll need to press Up at the foot of the stairs and down at the top of the stairs to move up and down. Be careful at the top of the stairs! You'll fall straight down if you simply walk forwards without pressing Down to get onto the stairs.

Secret Tip

When you encounter the stairs, you'll see that there are three platforms that are connected by these stairs. The last platform's rightmost brick is breakable for a pickup.

Continue once you're comfortable with how stairs work in this game. Keep going right, past the 3 tall windows and pillars. Make your way up the final set of steps. You'll reach a door at the top of the stairs. This is the main objective of every stage: to get to this door.

Stage 2

You'll start off on a platform. Immediately, a Vampire Bat will be flying at you. Destroy it!

Look down at the bottom of the screen. There are a set of stairs leading into a gap in the floor. You want to get down those stairs into the basement.

To get there, move right and get down the first set of stairs to your right.

Secret Tip

There's a secret ham in the wall right at the foot of the stairs!

Head left and go down the stairs into the basement.

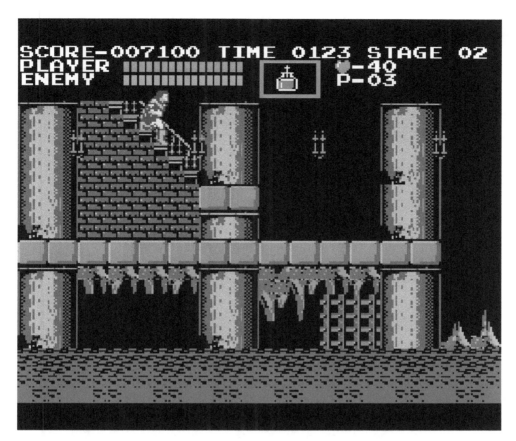

In the basement, beware the water: if you fall in you'll drown and die! Fishmen will also jump out of the water and onto the platform. You can destroy them with one shot with the Morning Star. Just be careful of the fireball that they spit at you.

Secret Tip

Break the last brick of the platform and kneel down at the two-brick platform below.

A money bag will pop up! Collect it and continue up the stairs on that platform.

Move left and jump over the platforms safely. Go up the stairs to exit the basement. At the ground floor, get up the stairs on the right and jump onto the platform to the right. Continue through the door to reach Stage 3.

Stage 3

Continue to the right, down the two sets of stairs and past the tall pillars. Keep an eye on the top of the screen—you'll see a bat perching there! You've reached the first boss!

BOSS BATTLE Phantom Bat

To the right side, you'll see two-brick platform and a set of stairs. You can break the right-most brick for a Double Shot, which enables you to throw weapons two times in a row.

The Phantom Bat's movements are somewhat random. It'll fly around and swoop down at you to attack you. Make sure that you don't let it touch you.

To keep safe, hide under the stairs: the Phantom Bat won't be able to move through those platform bricks. It's possible that it'll get in, but you remain in a defensible position and are able to whip him from where you are.

The safest and fastest way to defeat the Phantom Bat is to use Fire Bombs. As the Phantom Bat swoops in towards you, aim your Fire Bombs to land at the platform at the foot of the stairs. This will catch him in a fire and freeze him there. Continue throwing Fire Bombs until the Phantom Bat dies. If you don't have Fire Bombs, just be careful not to get hit by the bat and take every opportunity to damage it until you destroy it.

Congratulations on defeating your first Boss! Collect the Magic Crystal (shaped like a red orb) to replenish your health.

Note

All your hearts will be exchanged for points at the end of a Boss battle. Feel free to use up as many hearts as you like in order to defeat the boss. You'll start the next stage with 5 hearts.

You'll be shown a map after this boss battle. Take a look at the map to orient yourself about how you'll be progressing through the game.

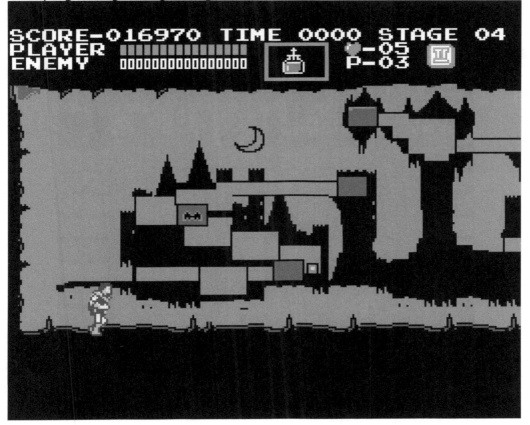

Stage 4

You're now ascending the tower of the castle.

In this stage, you'll encounter a new kind of enemy: the Black Knight. The Black Knight takes 2 hits with a Morning Star whip to defeat. Also, in this very first room, there are two Candlesticks with important items.

As soon as you enter through the door, you'll see a Candlestick overhead. You can choose to break this to collect the Boomerang weapon. At the top of this room is another Candlestick with a Triple Shot in it.

Go up the first set of stairs.

Secret Tip

On the first stairwell landing, you can break the wall on the right. Enter the space

to get a crown worth 2000 points to appear. Collect it and be on your way.

Then jump onto the platform that the Black Knight is standing on. Destroy the Black Knight and the Vampire Bat. Then, go up the stairs and destroy the Candlestick to collect a Triple Shot.

In this next room, you'll move to the left. Go up the stairs and jump onto this first platform.

Secret Tip

On the first platform that you jump onto (it has 6 bricks), you can destroy the leftmost brick for an item.

Make your way to the left. You may choose to jump over the Black Knight in the pit. Continue leftward and destroy another Black Knight. You'll arrive at a moving platform. Simply jump onto it and proceed through the door to reach the next stage. If you wish to be safe, drop onto the lower platform and jump straight up once the moving platform is above you. Then jump to the door.

Stage 5

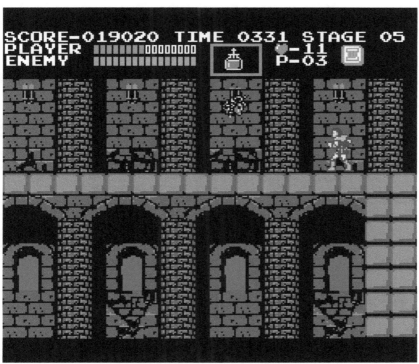

We are higher up in the castle tower now. Very quickly, you'll be introduced to the Medusa enemy. Beware of the wavy flight path: the path that the Medusa travels changes depending on where you are at the time that the enemy appears. It requires good timing to dodge or destroy them. It's advisable to just dodge them by watching their pattern for the upward movement, which gives you enough clearance to move forward. The flight path will change every time you move, so it pays to move in small increments and wait for the next Medusa to disappear off-screen before proceeding.

Continue moving right, past the pillars and windows, as quickly and safely as you can—the Medusas will continue appearing until you reach a certain point. You'll encounter a raised 2-brick platform that obstructs you. Jump over it and continue to the left until you reach the end and go up the stairs.

Get on that 2-brick platform and stand still for 2 seconds. A 2000-point treasure chest will appear to the right! Collect it and proceed left.

Look above you. That door is where you're trying to get to. You're going to go all the way to your right, use a platform to get to the upper level, and head left until you reach that door.

In front of you to the right, you'll see a series of 2-brick platforms. <u>CAUTION</u>: When the Medusas hit you, you'll most likely fall to your death! Duck in the middle of the first platform and watch their pattern. Be careful of stepping off the left side of the first platform: those stairs won't save you unless you press Down to get onto them! If you just walk to the left, you'll fall straight to your death!

The Medusas will continue to come at you. Destroy several Medusas until there is a safe window for you to jump onto the next platform. Or just time it carefully—stay close to the right edge of the platform and watch the Medusa carefully; as soon as it goes over your head, make your jump forwards.

Continue your careful jumps to the right-hand side and you'll reach a long stretch of solid platform. There will be a 2-brick platform at head level blocking your way. Jump on it, then jump up to the platform to the left with the Black Knight on it. Destroy him and continue to the left.

There's another 2-brick platform on a higher elevation this one, to the rights. The rightmost brick has a Pork Chop hidden inside!

As you continue to the left, take care to avoid taking damage from the Medusas. Don't be afraid to move backwards a little bit to avoid them before moving forwards to the left-hand side. Soon, you'll reach the door. Walk through it to continue to Stage 6.

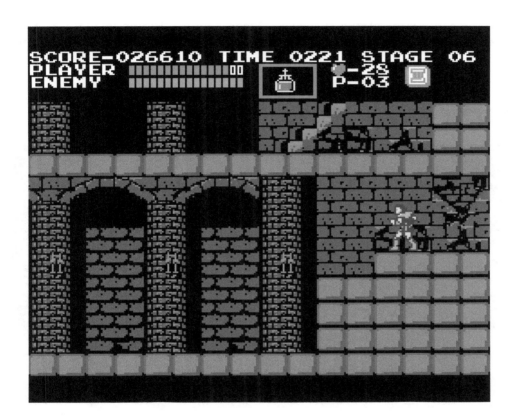

Stage 6

Look above you. See those stairs? You're going to be heading there. In this stage you'll move all the way to the left, move up to the upper level, and continue to the right until you reach those stairs.

In front of you are 3 pillars with Candlesticks on them. Destroy them and collect the pickups.

Moving forward, you'll encounter 3 crushing platforms moving up and down. Beware! They'll crush you if you're not careful. For each crusher, get as close to it as possible and wait to observe the timing. Make your move as soon as you see the second movement. Do this quickly and make sure to move just far enough so that you don't get your back crushed. The pillars are safe spaces.

Make your way to the left and you'll soon see Dragon Skull Cannons above. Be careful of the Ghost that'll be approaching from behind. It'll take 2 Morning Star hits to destroy.

Go up the stairs and destroy the Dragon Skull Cannons. They flash just before they shoot out two fireballs, then take about 4 seconds before they fire again. If you time it correctly, you can destroy the fireballs with your whip. The Dragon Skull Cannons take 6 hits to destroy, so be patient. The second one will be easy to destroy if wait just after it finishes firing to get onto the platform and duck (press Down) while you attack.

Continue forward and up the stairs to the next room.

Get up on that platform and continue to the left, passing the archways.

Soon, you'll reach a large statue, a bust of Queen Medusa. Hiding inside it is Queen Medusa herself. Move in front of the statue and move away to bring her out in the open and start the boss battle.

BOSS BATTLE Queen Medusa

Queen Medusa will fly around in a random movement pattern and will swoop in to hit you. She'll also drop snakes that will crawl towards you. Avoid the snakes and avoid Queen Medusa. She'll have moments where she pauses. You can use this moment to maneuver.

The best weapon to use here is the Fire Bomb: use the same bombing tactic. It'll take around 9 bombs, but don't be stingy about using them: you want to keep your advantage.

If you don't have Fire Bombs, use whatever you have at your disposal. You can defeat her even with just your Magic Whip. Hit her 2-3 times with your whip before moving away. When possible, retreat to the right, where there's an elevated platform. There, you'll find it easier to jump over Queen Medusa and run away from her. If you take damage, take advantage of the moment of protection that you'll get to run through her.

Destroy the Queen Medusa, collect the Magic Crystal, and move on to Stage 7.

Stage 7

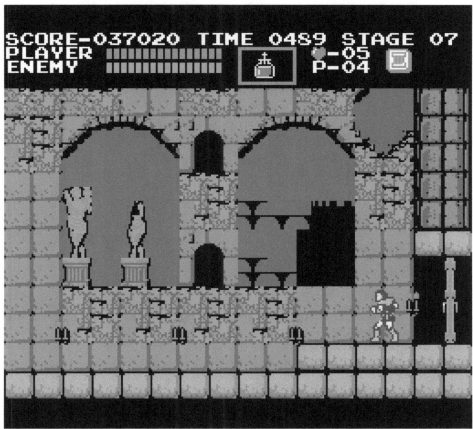

You start in a garden. In this stage, you'll move straight to the left and make your way to a staircase leading into the next room.

Move left and you'll see a low, 2-brick platform. Perched on top of it is the Hunchback enemy. The Hunchback enemy is fast and hops around, but is easy to kill. He alternates between moving along the ground in a straight predictable line and jumping in an arc. Kill the Hunchback and continue.

Pass under this first platform and you'll see a second platform with yet another Hunchback.

Secret Tip

In this second 2-brick platform, the leftmost brick has a Pork Chop hidden inside!

Continue to the left and you'll see a series of platform that lead up to the stairs. Beware the White Skeleton! He moves quickly and in bursts, and will throw bones at you. If you approach him, he'll generally move away from you.

Jump up the platforms and avoid the bones. Destroy the White Skeleton and make your way up the stairs to the next room.

Move up the stairs and drop down to the platform below. Continue to the right-hand side. Jump over the gap and go up the short steps. At that landing, you'll see that you can progress by jumping up onto the next platform or hopping down to the one below.

Secret Tip

If you touch the right half of the 4-brick platform, a Money Bag will appear on the left side!

Make your jumps across the platforms and go down the stairs (remember to press Down, otherwise you'll fall straight down to your death!). Go through the door to enter the next stage.

Stage 8

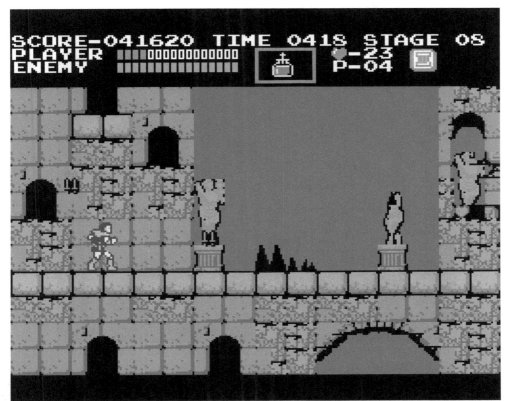

We are still outside the castle walls, high above the ground. Make your way across the walkway. If you keep moving forward, the Medusas that appear shouldn't need any dodging.

You'll come to a staircase. A White Skeleton will appear at the landing. Continue up the second set of stairs to the next room.

Secret Tip

If you duck at the first patch of plants on the wall, a money bag will appear on the left side!

Continue on the walkway and you'll encounter a Dragon Skull Cannon. Remember the timing and the warning signal that it gives before firing. Destroy it. Beware of the Ravens as well, who will swoop down to your level and fly at you in a straight line.

Next there will be a series of platforms to jump over. Avoid or kill the Ravens and you'll arrive at another Dragon Skull Cannon guarding the door to the next stage. Stand up and whip the cannon until it's destroyed—again, time it so that the fireballs will be destroyed as you whip the cannon. Then go through the door to progress to Stage 9.

Note

The Dragon Skull Cannons will turn to face you, so moving through them won't stop them from being a threat.

Stage 9

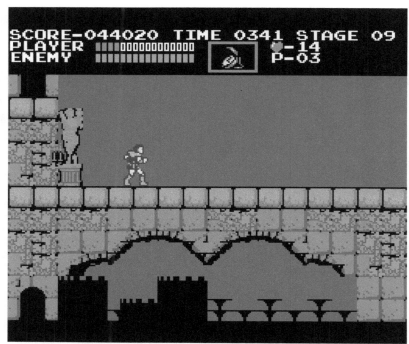

You're continuing on a long walkway high above the castle. Move to the right-hand side to make your way closer to the Count.

This walkway will be guarded by many Dragon Skull Cannons and Ravens. Kill the Ravens, otherwise they may become a nuisance when they attack you from behind while you're focused on hitting the Cannons.

You'll soon come to a series of gaps with a White Skeleton guarding the path. After you dispatch the White Skeleton and jump over these gaps, there will be yet another Dragon Skull Cannon. This time, it's guarded by Medusas, making this a tricky battle.

You'll have to be careful with the timing. Stay still while you whip forward so that you protect yourself from the Cannon's fireballs. Take small steps forward, don't be too ambitious. Once you destroy the Cannon, you can proceed safely into the castle interior, where you'll enter a chamber with a mummy in it.

BOSS BATTLE Mummy Man

The two Mummies will come to life shortly after you reach the middle of the chamber. They will walk towards you and fling their mummified bandages at you. Avoid them and their bandages.

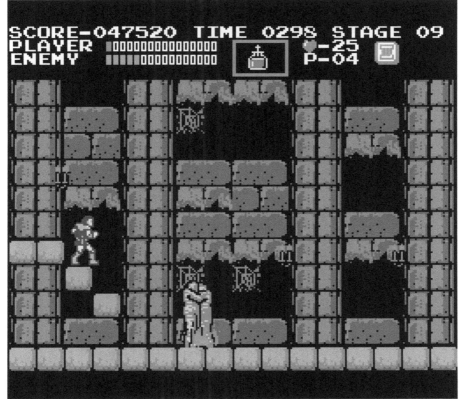

The easiest way to beat this boss is to stay above the Mummies by standing on the platform and toss Fire Bombs down below. If you don't have any bombs, then you'll have to fight them on the ground level. Do your best to keep the Mummies on one side, that way you can damage them both in one shot with your whip, and also to reduce the likelihood of getting hit from both sides.

If you're in trouble and need health, there is a Pork Chop hidden in the lowest 'step' of the platform bricks that lead down into the chamber.

Destroy the Mummies and make your way to Stage 10!

Stage 10

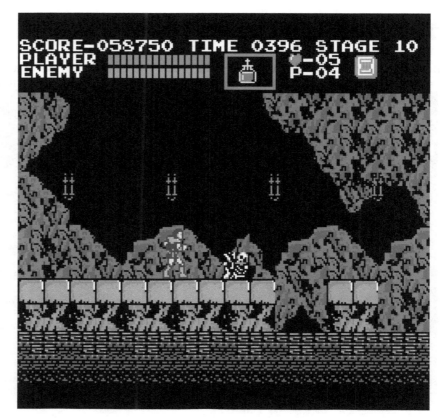

You're getting closer to the Count! You are now in a cave, with deadly water below. Beware of the Vampire Bats: you may have to duck to whip them. Ducking will become a good habit for this stage. The Fish Man makes a return as well.

Make your way across the gaps and moving platforms. You'll come across a series of short platforms that lead you up to a longer platform made of four bricks. Drop off of it onto the 2-brick platform. Edge forwards to get the Vampire Bat to come towards you, otherwise it may hit you on your jump to the moving platform ahead. CAUTION: the skulls are not a platform that you can step on!

Duck while you're on the platform, otherwise the stalactites overhead will knock you off the platform and you'll drown. You'll reach a stationary platform. Get onto it safely and drop onto the next moving platform and immediately Duck.

Continue forward up the stairs and into the next stage.

Stage 11

You have emerged from that dangerous cave! There won't be any treacherous gaps to jump over in this stage, but now the threats come from above. The Count is sending Eagles to drop Hunchbacks to stop you. You won't have much time to admire the lush greenery here.

As you move to the right-hand side, keep an eye out for Eagles and do your best to destroy the Hunchback before he lands. Otherwise, you'll quickly be overwhelmed by how many of them there are. You'll have to look both left and right.

Continue to the right. You'll eventually reach a door. It's guarded by a Skele-Dragon!

The Skele-Dragon will move its head up and down and spit a fireball at you. The simplest way to defeat the Skele-Dragon is by tossing Fire Bombs at it. Don't be worried about using your weapons: each Skele-Dragon will give you plenty of hearts when you kill it.

If you don't have any or don't want to use them, simply time your whips to destroy the fireball that the Skele-Dragon fires at you.

Destroy the Skele-Dragon and continue through the door to the next room.

This room consists of a long narrow corridor. You'll encounter two more Skele-Dragons. Then you'll reach a tall chamber. On the right side, you'll see Frankenstein and Igor.

Secret Tip

On the ledge before you drop into the chamber, you can destroy the brick on the left side for an item.

BOSS BATTLE Frankenstein & Igor

Frankenstein will move towards you slowly, and Igor will jump around and shoot fireballs at you. Those fireballs can be destroyed with your weapons. Damaging either Igor or Frankenstein will be effective at beating this boss.

As with nearly all the Bosses, Fire Bombs are the easiest way to kill Frankenstein & Igor. If you don't have any, focus on Igor because he is faster and shooting fireballs at you. Don't stay in the same spot, always strike and then move. Frankenstein is slow, so don't worry too much about him. Continue damaging the boss until you've defeated them. Then collect your Magic Crystal to continue to the next stage.

Stage 13

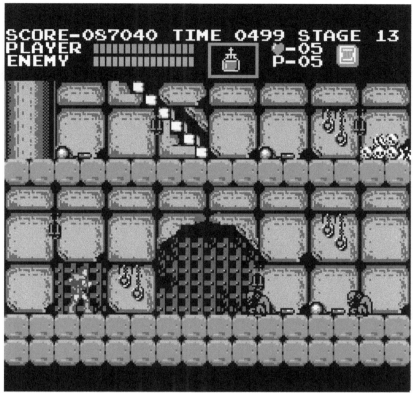

You're now in the Count's dungeon! Look above you and you'll see stairs that lead to another room. To get there, you'll be moving to the right and taking the stairs to the upper level, then moving left to reach those stairs.

Quickly take care of the Hunchbacks and head to the right. Head up the stairs to the upper level and destroy the White Skeletons. Continue to the left where you'll be met by the staircase that you saw earlier. Take these stairs up into the next room.

In this next room, be careful not to get hit by the bones that the White Skeletons are throwing. Keep an eye out for the one on the upper level—the bones can make it through and hit you.

Take the stairs that lead to the upper level of this room and continue right, then go down the stairs.

Secret Tip

Keep going past the steps instead of down the stairs, and keep walking right, into the wall. After 2-3 seconds, a 1-Up will appear down below! Be quick though. Once you descend onto the landing below, simply walk left to drop down into the pit to collect it.

Head down the stairs and continue to the right. You'll encounter the Red Skeleton. This enemy doesn't permanently die—it'll come right back to life after 3 seconds of dying. Kill the Red

Skeletons so that you can focus on destroying the Hunchbacks. Continue forward and you'll reach the door to the next stage.

Stage 14

You've made your way to the Count's laboratory! Immediately, you'll encounter two Axe-Men and a Hunchback. The Axe-Man will throw axes at you. These axes move in a straight horizontal line for a certain distance and then return to the Axe-Man, just like a boomerang. They throw these axes at different heights: you can duck some of them, but also throw them at foot level as well, so be careful. Their axes can be destroyed by your whip. The Axe-Man will move away from you. To get rid of him, you can simply move towards him cautiously—whip any axes that he throws at you—until he disappears off the edge of the screen. He's heavily armored, so it'll take a lot of your resources to kill him. It's best to just avoid him and move on.

Take care of the first Axe-Man, head up the stairs, and dispatch the second one. Continue up the stairs and into the next room.

In this next room, head up the stairs towards the coffins. Beware the Red Skeleton. Continue to the left until you reach the white staircase.

Secret Tip

At the landing, drop to the right where you see lab equipment. Stand still between the two red bins. A Money Bag will appear to the left!

Head to the left and be careful of the Axe-Man. Throwing a weapon at him will be the safest way to defeat him. Make sure to whip the axes that come at you.

Continue leftwards and you'll see a 2-brick platform with stairs leading to the upper level.

Secret Tip

Hop over the 2-brick platform and stand still at the left-hand corner of the dungeon cage (the grid of red metal strips). A Money Bag will appear to the right!

Get onto the upper level and you'll encounter an Axe-Man to the left. Head in that direction and whip the Axe-Man every time he throws an axe at you. Continue and you'll see a staircase. Head down (be careful of the Red Skelton) to the door to the next stage.

Stage 15

Immediately, a Dragon Skull Cannon will begin firing at you. Destroy it. You'll see a staircase on the upper level. This is where you want to go. Continue to the left.

You'll see a staircase leading to the upper level. Up there, a Dragon Skull Cannon and Red Skeleton is on guard. The Candlestick under this staircase should yield a Weapon—this is a chance for you to switch your weapon if you don't like the one you have.

Get onto the staircase and go up just enough so that your head is below the top edge of the upper platform. Wait until the moment the Red Skeleton is walking to the right. Then move up the stairs just enough so that your head is on the same level as the top of the bottom dragon skull on the cannon. This will let you whip the cannon without risking your health. Destroy the Dragon Skull Cannon and beware the Red Skeleton. Continue to the right, and you'll arrive at the stairs that you saw in the beginning. Go upstairs into the next room.

Secret Tip

Move past the stairs to the right and destroy the wall to get a Porkchop! You'll need it!

You've reached a chamber with lush red curtains. CAUTION: as soon as you emerge from the stairs, a Medusa will come out from the right-hand side. Resist the urge to move left or right and instead stay still at the spot right where you came up from the stairs.

Once the Medusa passes, head left and dispatch the Axe-Man. Move in small increments and find a safe spot where you can stand without being hit by the Medusas. Throw your Weapon at the Axe-Man until you destroy him.

Continue to the left and make sure to destroy the Candlesticks. You'll pick up a Double Shot and even a Triple Shot. Pass the empty picture frames and you'll encounter two tall pillars with a long platform in the middle and two short elevated platforms to the left and right of that middle platform. Prepare yourself for a Boss Battle!

BOSS BATTLE *Grim Reaper*

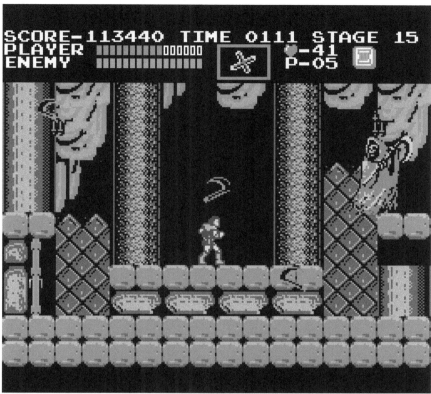

Brace yourself—this is going to be a tough battle!

The Grim Reaper will appear on the upper-right platform and 3-4 spinning scythes will appear. These scythes will continue appearing and will move towards you, pause momentarily, and continue moving towards you. The Grim Reaper himself will float from platform to platform.

Manage the threats by destroying 2-3 of the scythes, leaving only one of them to dodge. Use that time window to throw your Weapon at the Grim Reaper. Try to stay on the left or right edge of the middle platform. That way you can hop onto the upper platforms when you're getting overwhelmed by the scythes.

If you're using a Boomerang, stand on the middle platform and fire as many as you can at that level, preferably from either edge towards the other edge (e.g. stand on the left edge and fire to the right). This will free up your attention to whip any scythes that might get through the Boomerangs. The Grim Reaper will be damaged when he floats onto the middle platform. An alternative strategy is to draw the Grim Reaper into the middle platform, jump onto the upper-left platform, and fire Boomerangs at him. This will give you vertical space to evade the scythes.

No matter what weapon you use, try to give yourself breathing room by destroying a few scythes. Note: they only move so far before pausing to assess your latest position. You can exploit this by luring the scythes to the middle position and jumping to the upper platform.

Destroy the Grim Reaper and move on to the next stage.

You've climbed all the way up to the top of the castle!

There's a Candlestick above your head at this doorway that you came out of. Get the Axe from it if you want. The Axe, with its vertical arc, will be useful at attacking enemies when they're above you. Remember that you may want to keep your Fire Bomb or preferred weapon for a later Boss Battle.

Take the first set of stairs to the left and make your way leftwards across the walkway. Beware the Phantom Bats. They will fly towards you and fire fireballs at you. It's easiest to simply continue past them instead of trying to destroy them. They appear at two elevations above or below you, so get close to them so that they make their first move. Once they make that first move, they'll pause to consider their next move. Use this pause to your advantage and continue past them without any hassle.

Jump over the gaps on the walkway and avoid confronting the Phantom Bats. You'll soon arrive at a doorway that leads back into the castle interior.

You're now inside the clock tower. You'll see a White Skeleton tossing bones at you from across the gap. Destroy him and continue up the two sets of stairs into the next room.

You'll emerge onto a landing to the right. CAUTION: don't simply walk to the left or you'll fall to your death! Remember to jump across the stairs to the left.

Engage the White Skeleton at your level. Be careful not to get hit by the bones, otherwise you might get pushed into the gap and fall to your death. Continue up the stairs onto the upper level and make your way to the left.

Eagles will swoop in from the sides and drop off some Hunchbacks. Be careful: the Hunchbacks can climb the stones beneath you! You'll soon arrive at the gears of the clock tower.

You can walk on the gold-colored gears that are laid down horizontally, and you can walk through the vertical golden spokes.

Secret Tip

Drop down to the lowest gear and break the wall to your right. There's a Porkchop in there.

Continue left and you'll see a platform with two sets of stairs. Go down the stairs.

At the landing, drop down to your left to the platform below and continue left on the stairs. Be careful of the Eagles flying left and right when you go up the stairs. You'll continue moving up until you get back outside.

Stage 18

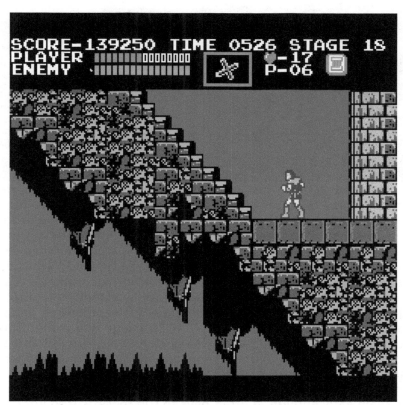

You're finally here to confront the Count! You'll see green mossy stairs. Go up them and head left into the Count's chambers. Move past the tall windows and you'll soon see the Count's coffin. Move past it and destroy the Candlestick on the left side of this chamber to arm yourself with the Fire Bomb.

A masked face will appear on the right-hand side and rise. The Count now appears!

BOSS BATTLE The Count

This is the moment that you've been working so hard to arrive at! It's time to destroy the Count!

The Count opens his cape to throw fireballs at you. Three fireballs are fired each time: they come at you fairly quickly in a spreading pattern. The fireballs must hit your torso to count as a hit. After the Count fires, he'll disappear briefly and teleport right onto your position. He'll telegraph his new position by appearing and flashing, giving you a brief moment to prepare.

To destroy the Count, you must strike his head—striking his body won't do anything. When the Count appears, keep approximately one square between you and him. Use the squares on the floor as a guide. Wait for him to open his cape: it can be tempting to strike before he does, but resist that urge and you'll be rewarded. The moment his cape opens, jump and strike at his head. The timing must be precise. Master it and you'll damage him without taking any damage yourself. If he is too far away, don't get aggressive. Stand your ground and simply time a full jump to avoid the fireballs. Continue to do this. It's not advisable to waste your weapons here.

Sometimes, the Count will appear far from you. Stay where you are, don't try to run to him to hit him. Let him launch his fireballs at you. Note that it's instinctive to run away from the fireballs. If you see them early enough, it often pays to run towards it to jump over them.

Once you whip the Count's head enough to deplete his health to zero, the Count's head will fly off and he'll transform into his beast form.

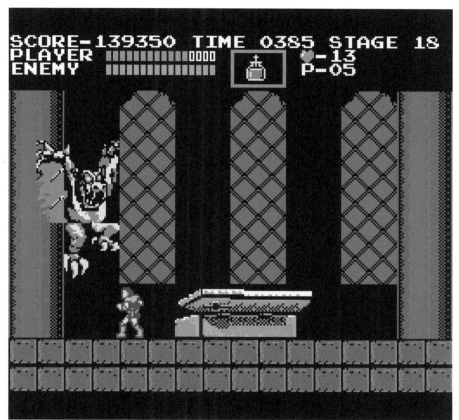

The Count will transform into a winged beast. He can jump in varying heights, from low jumps to high jumps. His jumps are meant to crush you: he will land where you were just prior to the jump. He can also shoot fireballs from his snout. If you destroy the fireballs, there's a chance that you can pick up an item.

The surefire way to defeat the Count's beast form is to stay close to him and be patient. By staying close to the Count, he'll most likely perform a high jump. This gives you a chance to make a short movement in the direction that he jumped from (basically you're moving under him when he jumps). Stay near the middle so that way you don't get cornered. Once he lands, jump and throw a Fire Bomb at his head. This will freeze him and you can whip his head as well. Continue this until he dies.

VICTORY The Ending

CONGRATULATIONS. You've defeated the Count and crumbled his castle!

The credits will appear. Pat yourself on the back: you defeated countless enemies and finally destroyed the Count himself.

Secret Tip

You can continue to the play the game after the credits roll. You'll start in Stage 1, but the stage counter reads Stage 19!

From one gamer to another please take a minute and write a review on the Amazon page for me.

Positive reviews help others purchase and enjoy theses books as well and I LOVE reading them too ☺

If you have any further questions or comments please reach me at blacknesguy@gmail.com
Twitter @blacknesguy
facebook.com/theBlackNESguy

To leave a review go here:

http://bit.ly/blacknesguy
****

Player 2 Press Start

It's dangerous to go alone. Take this... book for free.

Would you like to get the next book from BlackNES Guy for FREE?

Join my **Player 2 Press Start** team and I'll send you a copy of my next book (ebook) free of charge. The only thing that I ask in return is that if you like it that you please leave a review for it ☺

Game On!

http://bit.ly/Player2startnow

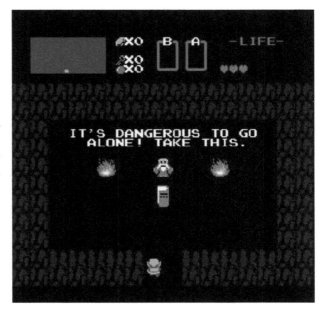

CPSIA information can be obtained
at www.ICGtesting.com
Printed in the USA
LVHW062122110219
607195LV00003B/18/P